W9-APH-705

SPIRITUALS

for piano · für Klavier · pour piano

Composed by
Komponiert von
Composé par

Péter Wolf

Könemann Music Budapest

K 166

INDEX

DEEP RIVER

Deep _____ Ri - ver, My home is o - ver Jor - dan, _____

Deep _____ Ri - ver, Lord I want to cross o - ver in - to camp ground.

Lord I is a com - in' Lord I is a com - in' I

want to cross o - ver in - to camp ground _____ I want to cross o - ver in - to camp ground.

JOSHUA FIT THE BATTLE OF JERICO

GO DOWN MOSES

Go down Mos - es 'Way down in E - gypt land ___ Tell ole Pha - roah

Let my peo - ple go. go. When Is - real was in E - gypt land Let my peo - ple

go. Oppres - sed so hard they could not stand Let my peo - ple go. Go down

Mos - es 'Way down in E - gypt land ___ Tell ole Pha - roah Let my peo - ple go.

16   K 166

GIVE ME THAT OLD TIME RELIGION

Give me that old time re - lig - ion, Give me that old time re -

lig - ion, Give me that old time re - lig - ion, It's good e - nough for me. ___

It was good for the He - brew chil - dren, It was good for the He - brew chil - dren, It was
It will bring you ___ out of bond - age, It will bring you ___ out of bond - age, It will

good for the He - brew chil - dren, And it's good e - nough for me. ___ Give me that
bring you ___ out of bond - age, And it's good e - nough for me. ___

Allegro

NOBODY KNOWS THE TROUBLE I'VE SEEN

No - bod - y knows the trou ble I've seen, No - bod - y knows but Je - sus.

No - bod - y knows the trou ble I've seen, Glor - y Hal - le - lu - jah! Some - times I'm up, some -

times I'm down Yes! Yes! Lord some - times I'm al - most to the ground Yes! Yes! Lord!

'ZEKIEL SAW THE WHEEL

'Ze - kiel saw the wheel, 'Way up in the mid - dle of the air,

'Ze - kiel saw the wheel, 'Way in the mid - dle of the air, The

big wheel run by faith, Lit - tle wheel run by the grace of God,

Wheel with - in a wheel, 'Way in the mid - dle of the air.

Wheel, wheel, wheel, wheel in the mid-dle of the air. Wheel, wheel, wheel, wheel in the mid-dle of the air.

SOMETIMES I FEEL LIKE A MOTHERLESS CHILD

Some-times I feel like a moth-er-less child, Some-times I feel like a moth-er-less child,

Some-times I feel like a moth-er-less child, A long ways from home, A long ways from

home, True be-liev-er, A long ways from home, A long ways from home.

Andante, cantabile

DOWN BY THE RIVERSIDE

IT'S A ME, O LORD

WERE YOU THERE

52

I WANT TO BE READY

ROLL JORDAN ROLL

Roll, Jor-dan Roll, Roll, Jor-dan Roll, I want to go to Heav-en when I die, to

hear Jor-dan Roll. hear Jor-dan Roll. Oh, Broth-ers you ought to been there

Yes, my Lord a - sit - tin' in the King - dom Hear Jordan Roll.

MICHAEL ROWS THE BOAT

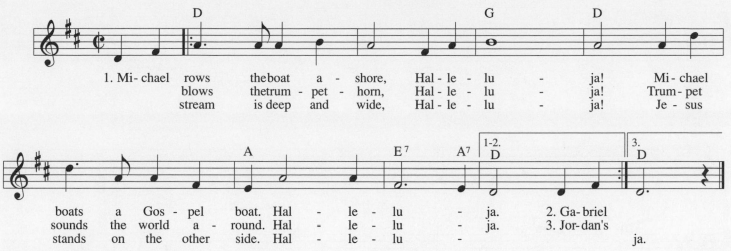

1. Mi - chael rows the boat a - shore, Hal - le - lu - ja! Mi - chael
blows the trum - pet horn, Hal - le - lu - ja! Trum - pet
stream is deep and wide, Hal - le - lu - ja! Je - sus

boats a Gos - pel boat. Hal - le - lu - ja. 2. Ga - briel
sounds the world a - round. Hal - le - lu - ja. 3. Jor - dan's
stands on the other side. Hal - le - lu - ja.

I'VE BEEN IN THE STORM SO LONG

I've been in the storm so long, I've been in the storm so long, chil-dren, I've
been in the storm so long, Oh give me lit-tle time to pray. ___ I've pray. ___ Oh I'll

let me tell my moth-er, ___ how I come a-long, Oh give me lit-tle time to pray, ___ With a
go ___ in-to heav-en, and take ___ my ___ seat, Oh give me lit-tle time to pray, ___ And a

hung down head and an ach-ing heart, Oh give me lit-tle time to pray. ___ I've
cast my crown at ___ Je-sus feet, Oh give me lit-tle time to pray. ___

been in the storm so long, I've been in the storm so long, chil-dren, I've

been in the storm so long, Oh give me lit-tle time to pray.

HE'S GOT THE WHOLE WORLD IN HIS HANDS

He's got the whole world ___ in His hands; ___ He's got the whole wide world ___

in His hands; ___ He's got the whole world ___ in His hands; ___ He's got the whole world in His

hands. He's got the earth and sky ___ in His hands; ___ He's got the

night and day ___ in His hands; ___ He's got the sun and moon ___

in His hands; ___ He's got the whole world in His hands. He's got the

Moderato

K 166

SWING LOW, SWEET CHARIOT

© 1995 for this edition by Könemann Music Budapest Kft.
H-1093 Budapest, Közraktár utca 10.

K 166/3

Distributed worldwide by
Könemann Verlagsgesellschaft mbH, Bonner Str. 126.
D–50968 Köln

Responsible co-editor: János Gyulai Gaál
Production: Detlev Schaper
Cover design: Peter Feierabend
Technical editor: Dezső Varga
Engraved by Apple computer: Katalin Énekes

Printed by Kossuth Printing House Co., Budapest
Printed in Hungary

ISBN 963 8303 90 5